Crafts for Halloween

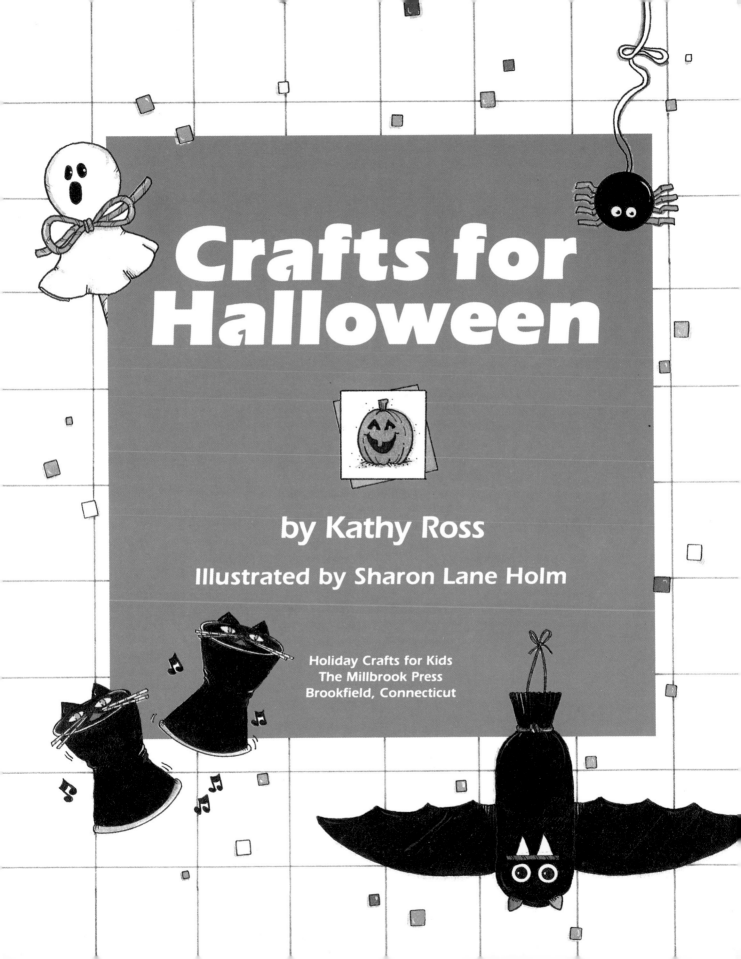

Crafts for Halloween

by Kathy Ross

Illustrated by Sharon Lane Holm

Holiday Crafts for Kids
The Millbrook Press
Brookfield, Connecticut

For Greyson and Allison

Library of Congress Cataloging-in-Publication Data
Ross, Kathy (Katharine Reynolds), 1948-
Crafts for Halloween/ by Kathy Ross;
illustrated by Sharon Lane Holm.
p. cm. —(Holiday crafts for kids)
Presents 20 simple craft projects, from
puppets to party favors, that young children
can make from everyday materials.
ISBN 1-56294-411-8 (lib. bdg.) ISBN 1-56294-741-9 (pbk.)
1. Halloween decorations—Juvenile literature.
2. Handicraft—Juvenile literature. [1. Halloween
decorations. 2. Handicraft.] I. Holm, Sharon
Lane, ill. II. Title. III. Series.
TT900.H32R67 1994
745.594'1—dc20 93-37249 CIP AC

Published by The Millbrook Press
2 Old New Milford Road
Brookfield, Connecticut 06804

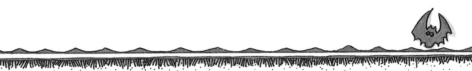

Contents

Happy Halloween!

On October 31, children in America celebrate Halloween. They dress up in costumes and go from house to house, asking for candy by saying "trick or treat." Some costumes are scary, some are silly, and others may be quite beautiful.

Long ago, people believed that spirits called ghosts wandered the earth, and they were afraid of these ghosts. Many of today's Halloween customs have come from this old belief. Carved pumpkins and scary costumes were once used to try to frighten the spirits away. Today people place lighted pumpkins on their porches to welcome the children in their costumes.

Witches casting spells and flying around on broomsticks with their black cats, screeching owls, spiders, and swooping bats are all considered symbols of this spooky celebration. Halloween is a holiday for having a scary good time.

Sock Pumpkin

Pumpkins with carved faces and glowing candles inside are called jack-o'-lanterns. Here are some pumpkins that you can make.

Here is what you need:

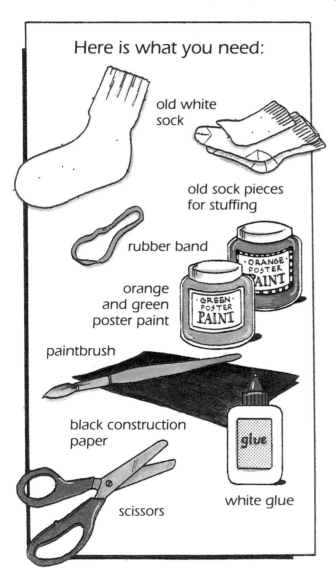

old white sock

old sock pieces for stuffing

rubber band

orange and green poster paint

paintbrush

black construction paper

white glue

scissors

Here is what you do:

1. Cut the toe half off the foot of the sock. Use the rest of the sock, and more sock pieces if you need them, to stuff the toe to form a round pumpkin. Secure the top with a rubber band, leaving the top of the sock sticking out for the stem.

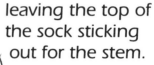

2. Paint the pumpkin orange and the stem green. Twist the stem while it is wet so it will dry in the shape of a stem. When the paint is dry, glue on a jack-o'-lantern face cut from black paper.

GREEN POSTER PAINT

ORANGE POSTER PAINT

glue

The size of each pumpkin you make will be determined by the size of the sock it is made from. Several stuffed pumpkins can be displayed together with green yarn and paper leaves entwined among them to look like a pumpkin patch.

Pumpkin Numbers Game

Here is what you need:

five bottle caps

orange poster paint

paintbrush

scraps of black and green construction paper

scissors

white glue

paper cup

Here is what you do:

1. Cut a black circle to fit inside each cap, and glue the circles in.

2. Mix a few drops of glue with orange paint in a paper cup. If you are using poster paint, you will also need to add a squirt of liquid dish soap to the mixture to help it stick to the metal caps. Paint the top and sides of the five caps with this mixture.

3. Cut tiny jack-o'-lantern faces from black paper and stems from green paper for the five caps. Set the faces and stems on the cap while the paint and glue mixture is still wet. Let the pumpkins dry before you play the game.

To play the pumpkin numbers game, take turns tossing the pumpkins on the floor or table. For each pumpkin that lands with the face showing, you get one point. You do not get a point for pumpkins that land face down. Keep track of how many points each player gets by writing the score down on a piece of paper. After five turns each, the player with the most points wins.

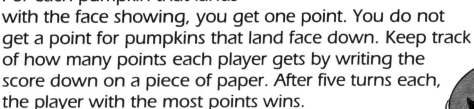

Talking Pumpkin Puppet

Ask an adult to help you make this pumpkin puppet.

Here is what you need:

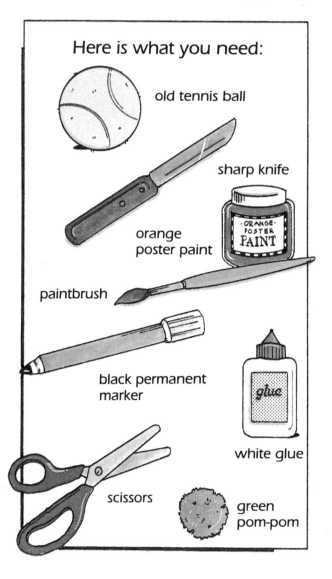

old tennis ball

sharp knife

orange poster paint

paintbrush

black permanent marker

white glue

scissors

green pom-pom

Here is what you do:

1. A slit needs to be cut in the bottom half of the tennis ball using a sharp knife. You may need an adult to help you with this. The cut will form the pumpkin's mouth.

2. Paint the tennis ball orange and let it dry.

3. Use a black marker to draw a mouth around the slit cut in the ball, and add a pumpkin nose and eyes. Glue a green pom-pom on top of the ball for a stem. To make your pumpkin talk just place a finger on each side of the mouth and squeeze. The mouth will open and close when you do this.

Talking pumpkins make great party favors because they can be filled through the cut mouth with candy and small surprises.

Milk Carton Witch

Witches like to turn people into toads, but you can turn a milk carton and an egg carton into a witch.

Here is what you need:

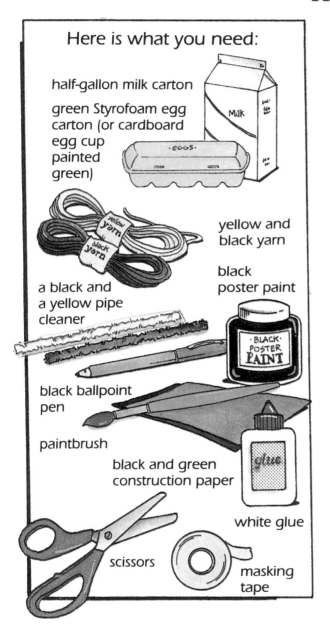

half-gallon milk carton

green Styrofoam egg carton (or cardboard egg cup painted green)

yellow and black yarn

black poster paint

a black and a yellow pipe cleaner

black ballpoint pen

paintbrush

black and green construction paper

white glue

scissors

masking tape

Here is what you do:

1. Cut the top off the milk carton just below the place where it starts to fold in to form the spout. You will need the top part of the carton to make the witch. (Hint: Save the bottom to make the Haunted House Treat Carrier on page 22.) Paint the milk carton top with black paint. If you use poster paint, you will need to cover the surface with masking tape, or the paint will not stick.

2. Cut one cup from the egg carton. Push it partway through the open spout of the milk carton and glue it in place to form the witch's face. Poke a piece of yellow pipe cleaner through the middle of the face to make a nose. Then draw on eyes and a mouth using a ballpoint pen. Glue long pieces of unraveled black yarn around the face for hair.

3. Make a broom for the witch to hold by tying several pieces of yellow yarn to one end of a black pipe cleaner. Cut two hands from green construction paper. Glue them on the front of the witch, with the broom between them.

4. Trace around the back (open) portion of the witch on black paper. Cut out the square shape and glue it over the opening.

If you are giving your witch to someone as a gift, you can write a Halloween greeting on orange paper and glue it on the back of the witch. If you are using her as a party favor, she can be filled with goodies before you cover the back.

BOO!

Wobbly Witch

Here is what you need:

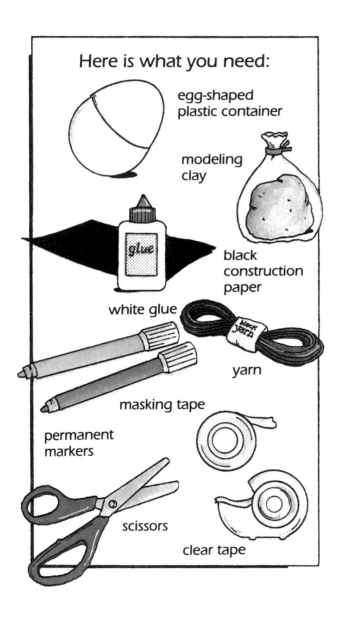

egg-shaped plastic container

modeling clay

black construction paper

white glue

yarn

masking tape

permanent markers

scissors

clear tape

Here is what you do:

1. Press enough clay into the bottom half of the egg to make it stand up when the top is placed back on it. Put two or three strips of masking tape in the bottom of the egg. Then glue the clay in place on top of the tape. Leave the egg open until it dries completely, and then put it together.

2.

Cut a semicircle from black paper and fold it into a cone for the witch's hat. Secure it with clear tape. Glue strands of unraveled yarn around half of the hat for hair, and tape the hat to the top of the egg. Cut a circle larger than the bottom of the hat for the brim. Cut an X-shaped slit in the center of the circle and carefully slide it over the point of the hat to form the brim. Tape it in place.

3.

Draw a witch face with the markers.

Push this witch over, and she will pop right up again.

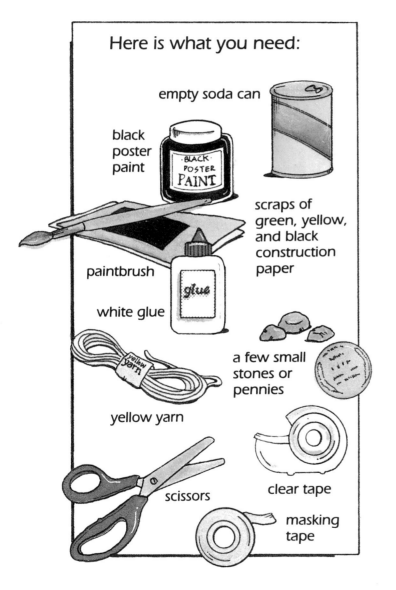

Can Cat Shaker

Witches like black cats for pets.

Here is what you need:

empty soda can

black poster paint

BLACK POSTER PAINT

scraps of green, yellow, and black construction paper

paintbrush

white glue

glue

yellow yarn

a few small stones or pennies

scissors

clear tape

masking tape

Here is what you do:

1. Drop a few stones or pennies into the can and put clear tape over the opening so they will not spill out when you shake the can.

2. If you are using poster paint, you will need to cover the sides and top of the can with masking tape, leaving the spout uncovered. Bend the soda can by placing it on the floor and stepping on it just below the spout in the top of the can. Paint the top and sides of the can black, and let the paint dry.

3. Cut eyes and ears from scrap paper and glue them in place above the opening of the can, which forms the cat's mouth. Make whiskers by knotting two pieces of yarn together in the middle and trimming the ends to the length you want the whiskers to be. Glue them on just above the mouth.

Shake your can cat in time to your favorite Halloween songs!

Yowling Cat Puppet

Here is what you need:

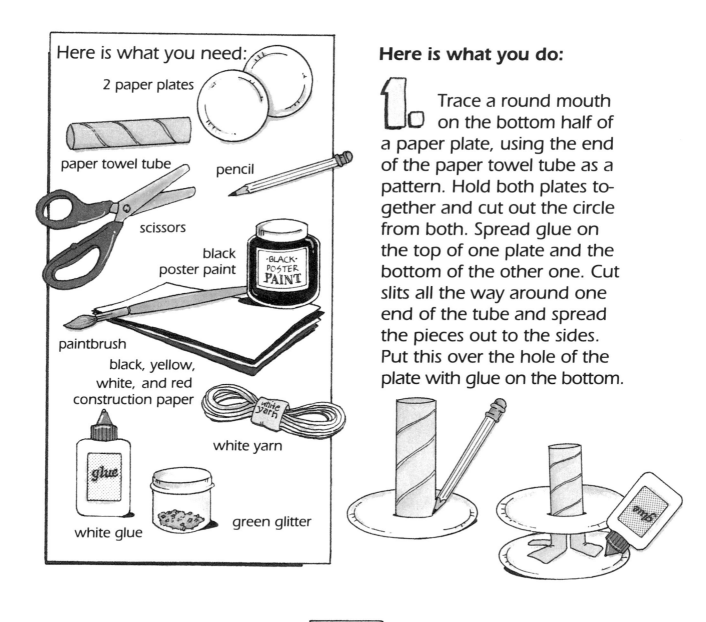

2 paper plates

paper towel tube

pencil

scissors

black poster paint

·BLACK· POSTER PAINT

paintbrush

black, yellow, white, and red construction paper

white yarn

white glue

glue

green glitter

Here is what you do:

1. Trace a round mouth on the bottom half of a paper plate, using the end of the paper towel tube as a pattern. Hold both plates together and cut out the circle from both. Spread glue on the top of one plate and the bottom of the other one. Cut slits all the way around one end of the tube and spread the pieces out to the sides. Put this over the hole of the plate with glue on the bottom.

Then slide on the other plate and press the two plates together so that the slit flaps are sandwiched between them. The tube will act as a megaphone to make your cat puppet yowl in a spooky way.

2. Wait until your puppet is completely dry before continuing. You may need to weight the plates with books to make sure they dry completely stuck together.

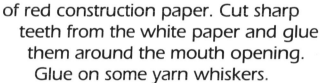

3. Paint the front of the puppet black. Cut triangle ears from black paper and glue them on. Cut cat eyes from yellow and black paper. To give them a very spooky look, use green glitter to make the centers. Glue a black pupil in the center of each eye. Line the mouth with a piece of red construction paper. Cut sharp teeth from the white paper and glue them around the mouth opening. Glue on some yarn whiskers.

After following steps one and two you might choose to make a different Halloween character, such as a bat, a witch, or a goblin Use your own ideas to create lots of different puppets.

Haunted House Treat Carrier

Make a haunted house for your Halloween goodies.

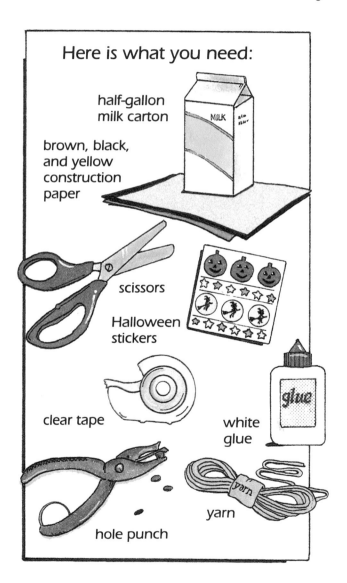

Here is what you need:

half-gallon milk carton

brown, black, and yellow construction paper

scissors

Halloween stickers

clear tape

white glue

hole punch

yarn

Here is what you do:

1. Cut the top off the milk carton just below the place where it starts to fold in to form the spout. You will need the bottom part for this project. Cover the carton with yellow paper cut to fit, and tape it in place.

2. Cut a piece of brown paper to cover the yellow paper. Hold it in place over the yellow paper and draw a front door and several windows. Remove the brown paper and cut the door and windows on three sides so that they open and shut. Tape the brown paper back in place over the yellow paper.

3. Cut nine long strands of yarn in one or more colors to make the handle. Punch two holes on opposite sides of the carton and tie the strings through one of the holes. Braid the strands together to make a strong handle for your treat carrier. Then knot the ends through the hole on the other side of the carton.

4. Open all your doors and windows and put a Halloween sticker inside each. Use a black marker to add details to the outside of your house. You may even want to put a ghost sticker or two on the outside to give it that haunted look. Cut a roof from black paper to glue on the front of the house.

You can draw your own spooky ideas for Halloween characters in your house instead of using Halloween stickers.

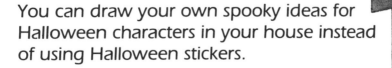

Floating Ghosts

Haunt your house with these Halloween ghosts.

Here is what you need:

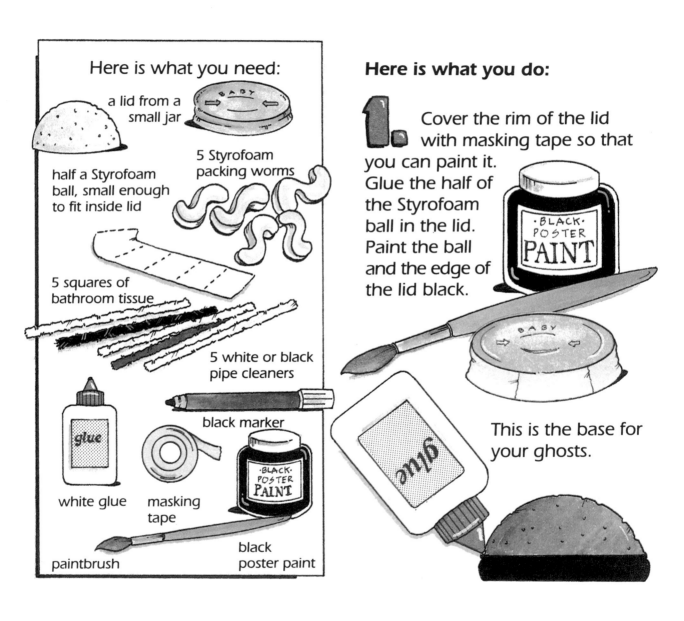

a lid from a small jar

half a Styrofoam ball, small enough to fit inside lid

5 Styrofoam packing worms

5 squares of bathroom tissue

5 white or black pipe cleaners

black marker

white glue

masking tape

paintbrush

black poster paint

Here is what you do:

1. Cover the rim of the lid with masking tape so that you can paint it. Glue the half of the Styrofoam ball in the lid. Paint the ball and the edge of the lid black.

This is the base for your ghosts.

2. To make each ghost, rub glue on the sides and end of a Styrofoam packing worm and loosely cover it with a square of bathroom tissue. Make five ghosts. Give each ghost a spooky face with a black marker.

3. Stick one end of a pipe cleaner into glue and then into the bottom of one of your ghosts. Stick the other end into the Styrofoam base. Do this with all your ghosts, and arrange them to look as if they are floating about.

Hairpin Ghost Necklace

Here is what you need:

plastic lid from margarine container or coffee can

hairpin

scraps of black construction paper

black thread

white glue

scissors

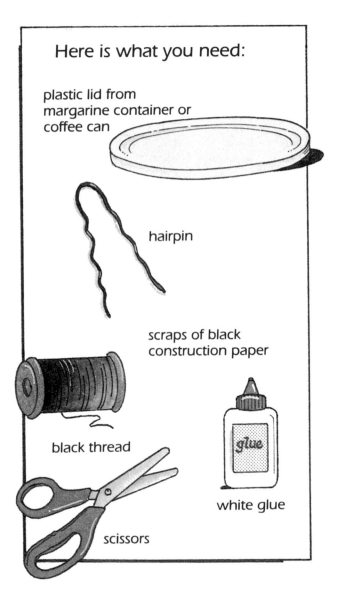

Here is what you do:

1. Spread the hairpin apart slightly so that it forms the outline of a ghost. Tie a long black thread around the top of the hairpin. Then tie the two ends of the thread together to make a necklace.

    26

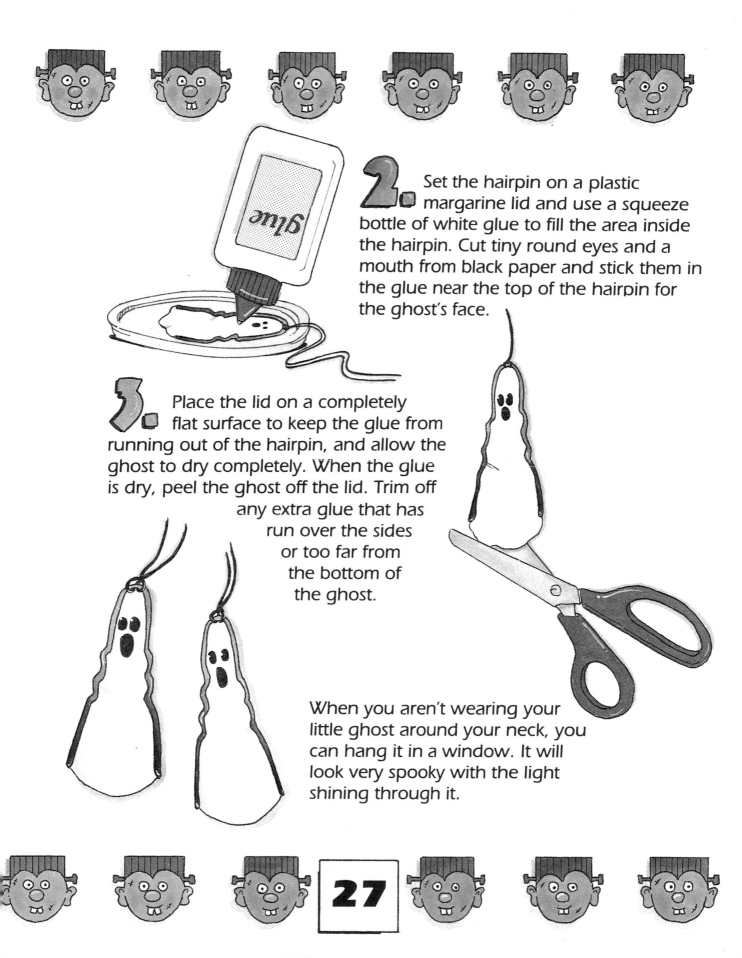

2. Set the hairpin on a plastic margarine lid and use a squeeze bottle of white glue to fill the area inside the hairpin. Cut tiny round eyes and a mouth from black paper and stick them in the glue near the top of the hairpin for the ghost's face.

3. Place the lid on a completely flat surface to keep the glue from running out of the hairpin, and allow the ghost to dry completely. When the glue is dry, peel the ghost off the lid. Trim off any extra glue that has run over the sides or too far from the bottom of the ghost.

When you aren't wearing your little ghost around your neck, you can hang it in a window. It will look very spooky with the light shining through it.

Transparent Ghost

Here is what you need:

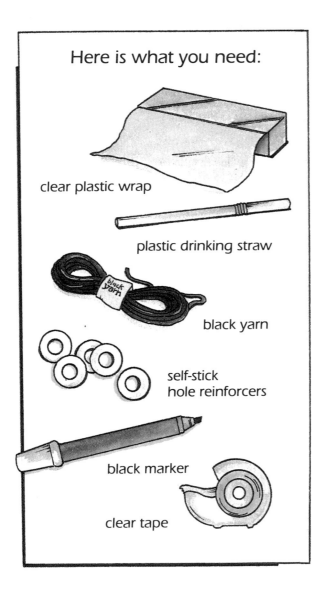

clear plastic wrap

plastic drinking straw

black yarn

self-stick
hole reinforcers

black marker

clear tape

Here is what you do:

1. Rip off a square of plastic wrap. Tie the wrap over the top of the straw so that it hangs down evenly around it to form a ghost. Blow up the head of the ghost through the straw. Carefully pull the straw out and tie the yarn tight in a bow to capture the air.

2. Color two hole reinforcers black and stick them on the head of the ghost for eyes. Tape a piece of yarn to the back of the ghost's head to hang it from the ceiling.

If your ghost loses air after a while, just insert the straw and blow it up again.

Pop-up Ghost Party Favor

Here is what you need:

round lollipop

white facial tissue

black yarn

plastic drinking straw

pudding or gelatin dessert box

gray construction paper

scissors

white glue

clear tape

black marker

Here is what you do:

1. Tie a tissue around the lollipop to make a ghost. Give him a spooky face with the black marker. Slide the lollipop stick into one end of a straw and secure it with tape.

30

2. Cut the flaps off the open (top) end of your box. Poke a hole through the bottom large enough to fit the straw. Cover the box with gray paper and tape it in place. Cut a tombstone shape to glue on the front of the box. Write something funny on the tombstone, using the name of the friend you will be giving the favor to.

3. Slide the straw down through the hole in the bottom of the box so that the ghost is hidden behind the tombstone. To make him pop out, just push up the bottom of the straw.

These make great candy favors for a Halloween party!

R.I.P. Mike

Little Ghost
Table Decoration

Here is what you need:

clear disposable plastic cup

two Styrofoam packing worms

green pipe cleaner

black construction paper

one square of bathroom tissue

black marker

orange permanent marker

scissors

white glue

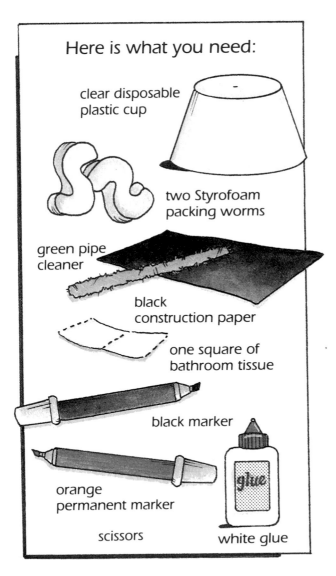

Here is what you do:

1. Trace around the rim of the cup on black paper, and cut the circle out.

2. Make the ghost by dipping one end of a Styrofoam packing worm in glue and then covering it with a square of bathroom tissue. Give the ghost a face with a black marker.

3. Make the pumpkin by cutting the end off another packing worm and coloring it orange. Poke a piece of green pipe cleaner in the top for the stem.

4. Glue the ghost and the pumpkin to the black circle. Let the glue dry completely before continuing. (If you don't, you will have moisture inside the cup.) Dip the rim of the cup in glue and set it over the circle so that the ghost and pumpkin are inside the cup.

If you store this decoration carefully you will have it to enjoy for many Halloweens to come.

Stuffed Sock Bat

Make a bat to hang around your house this Halloween.

Here is what you need:

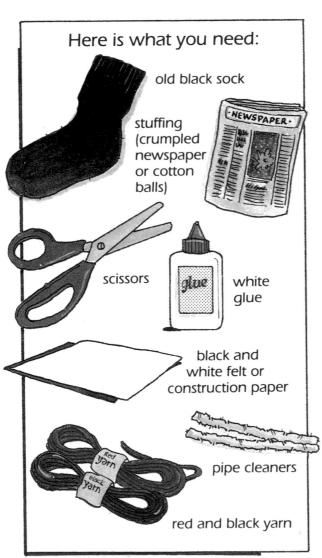

old black sock

stuffing (crumpled newspaper or cotton balls)

NEWSPAPER

scissors

white glue

black and white felt or construction paper

pipe cleaners

red and black yarn

Here is what you do:

1. Stuff the foot of a black sock and tie the end with black yarn. Tie the two ends of the yarn together so that you will be able to hang your bat upside down. Trim off the excess sock.

2. Cut eyes, ears, and teeth from the felt or paper and glue them at the toe end of the sock. Give your bat a smile cut from the red yarn. For each wing, cut a front and a back piece from the black felt or paper. Glue each front and back together with two or three pipe cleaners in between, so that the wings can be bent in different shapes. Glue the two wings to the back of your bat so that they stick out, and hang the bat upside down (bats' favorite position) to dry.

Spider Web

Eek! Spiders!

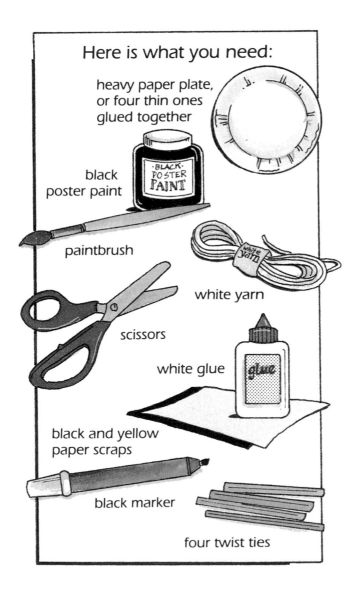

Here is what you need:

heavy paper plate, or four thin ones glued together

black poster paint

paintbrush

white yarn

scissors

white glue

black and yellow paper scraps

black marker

four twist ties

Here is what you do:

1. Cut several small slits, evenly spaced, around the edge of the paper plate. Paint the plate black. When it is dry, wrap white yarn around and around the plate to form a spider web, securing it in the slits around the edge. Leave one end of the yarn hanging off the web, so you will have a place to attach your spider. Tie the other end in a loop, so you can hang up your web.

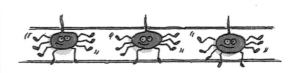

2. To make a spider, cut two circles of the same size from black paper. Cover one circle with glue and place four twist ties across the circle so that they stick out on each side to form the spider's legs. Add more glue, and cover the first circle with the second circle. Bend the twist ties to form knees and feet for the spider. Glue on eyes cut from yellow paper and draw a dot in the middle of each one with a black marker.

3. Attach your spider to the end of the yarn web by putting the loose end of the yarn between the two circles. Let the glue dry completely. Then hang your spider web on your front door. Your spider can hang out on his web or swing from it.

Spider Hat

Here is what you need:

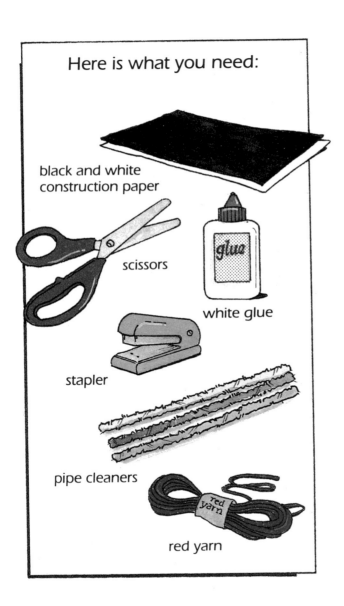

black and white construction paper

scissors

white glue

stapler

pipe cleaners

red yarn

Here is what you do:

1. Cut sixteen strips of black paper. To make each of the spider's eight legs, glue two strips together with a pipe cleaner in the middle. Staple the front and back of each leg together in three places so the pieces will hold together while the glue is drying.

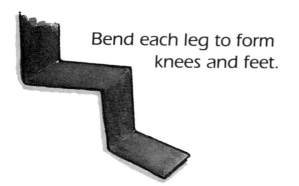

Bend each leg to form knees and feet.

2. Cut a black paper headband large enough to fit around your head. Cut a circle to make a head for the spider, and glue it to the middle of the headband. Add eyes cut from paper, and a red yarn smile.

3. Staple four legs on each side of the spider's head. Then staple the headband to fit your head.

Put on your hat and go find Miss Muffet.

Owl Message Can

Use this owl both day and night.

Here is what you need:

Popsicle sticks

cardboard can from frozen juice concentrate

wooden clothespin

brown and white construction paper scraps

white glue

brown and orange poster paint

paintbrush

white paper

pencil

Here is what you do:

1. Cover the outside of the can with glue. Then glue the Popsicle sticks all around the can to cover it. Break three sticks in half and glue them on each side of the can to form wings. Paint the sticks brown and let them dry.

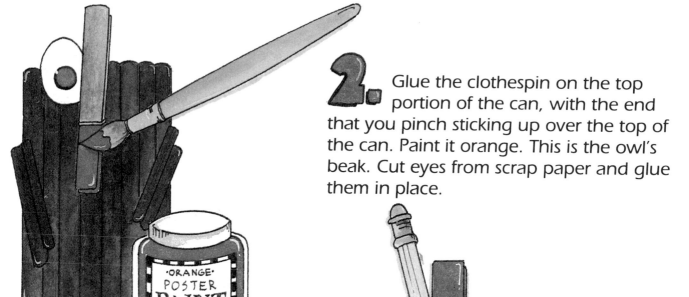

2. Glue the clothespin on the top portion of the can, with the end that you pinch sticking up over the top of the can. Paint it orange. This is the owl's beak. Cut eyes from scrap paper and glue them in place.

Put squares of white paper and a pencil inside the owl can. Messages can be clipped in the beak.

Happy Halloween!

Newspaper Owl

Here is what you need:

8 double sheets of newspaper, plus extra newspaper for stuffing

stapler

2 large and 2 small paper plates

paintbrush

brown, orange, and black poster paint

scissors

black and orange construction paper

white glue

Here is what you do:

1. Open eight double sheets of newspaper and stack them on top of each other. Staple them all together around the top, bottom, and one side, leaving the last side open like a bag. Open the newspaper bag up so that four sheets are on one side and four on the other. Stuff the bag with crumpled newspaper. Staple the open side shut.

2. Paint the newspaper owl brown on both sides. If you do not have a large paintbrush, you can use a sponge to spread the paint quickly.

3. To make the eyes, paint two small paper plates orange and glue one on top of each of the large paper plates. Cut two pupils for the eyes from black paper and glue one in the center of each of the orange plates. Glue the eyes on the top part of the owl. Cut a triangle beak from orange construction paper, and glue it on under the eyes. Use black paint to draw the outline of wings on each side of the owl's body.

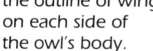

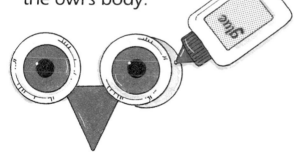

This owl is so big it will need a chair of its own!

Monster Man

Mad scientists make monsters in their laboratories.
You can make one, too!

Here is what you need:

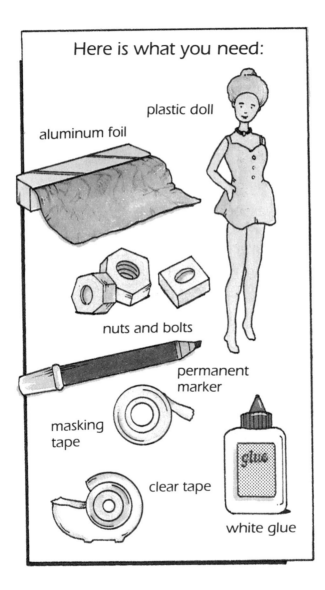

aluminum foil

plastic doll

nuts and bolts

permanent marker

masking tape

clear tape

white glue

Here is what you do:

1. Cover the doll completely with aluminum foil.

44

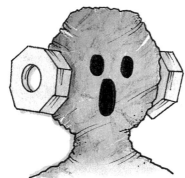

2. Glue on nuts and bolts for facial features and controls. Put a tiny piece of masking tape under each place where you want to glue so that the metal will stick better. Heavier bolts may need clear tape to hold them on. Use a permanent marker to add details.

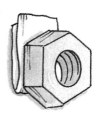

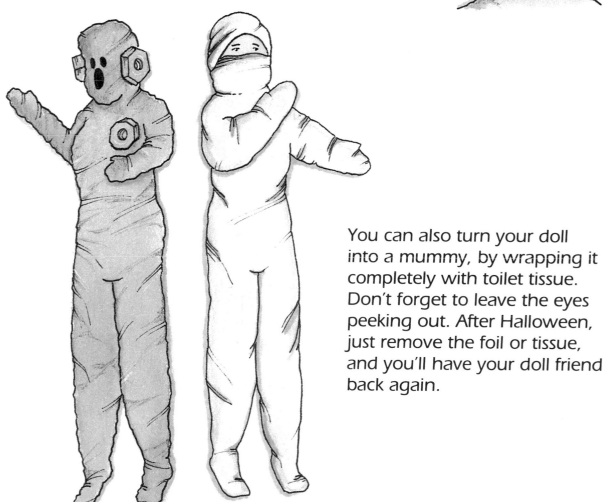

You can also turn your doll into a mummy, by wrapping it completely with toilet tissue. Don't forget to leave the eyes peeking out. After Halloween, just remove the foil or tissue, and you'll have your doll friend back again.

Goblin Game

Goblins are scary little monsters. Make your own scary monsters to play the goblin game.

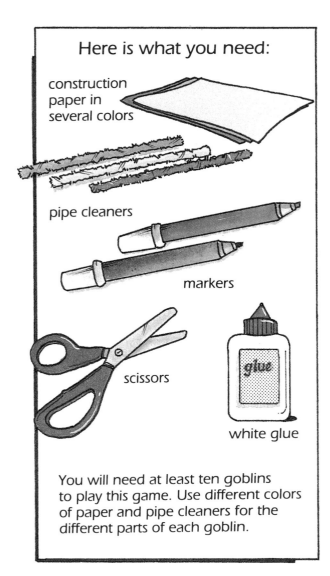

Here is what you need:

construction paper in several colors

pipe cleaners

markers

scissors

white glue

You will need at least ten goblins to play this game. Use different colors of paper and pipe cleaners for the different parts of each goblin.

Here is what you do:

1. For each goblin, cut two identical circles about the size of a quarter for the front and back of the head. Cut two larger circles for the front and back of the body. Cut two circles about half the size of the head for ears.

2. Cut three pipe cleaners in half to use for the arms, legs, and tail. You will need only five of these pieces for each goblin, so put one piece aside to use for your next goblin.

3. Spread glue all over one side of the large body circles and one side of the smaller head circles. Set the head on the edge of the body circle and put an ear circle on each side of the head so that they stick halfway out on each side. Set the five pieces of pipe cleaner in the glue on the large circle so that they stick out to form the goblin's arms, legs, and tail. Stick the second body circle over the first body circle, and the second head circle over the first head circle. The ends of the legs and tail should now be between the two sets of circles.

4. When all the goblins have dried, draw a crabby face on each one. Remember that goblins are usually angry. Bend all the arms, legs, and tails into hook shapes so that the goblins can hang from each other, and you are ready to play the game.

To play the Goblin Game, toss the goblins on the floor and take turns seeing how many of the goblins you can hook on in a row. You can hold only the first goblin, and your turn is over if any goblins drop off. Keep score to see who has hooked the most goblins after each player has had six turns.

 **47**

About the author and illustrator

Twenty years as a teacher and director of nursery school programs have given Kathy Ross extensive experience in guiding young children through craft projects. Her craft projects have appeared in **Highlights** magazine, and she has also written numerous songs for young children. She lives in Oneida, New York.

Sharon Lane Holm won awards for her work in advertising design before shifting her concentration to children's books. Her illustrations have since added zest to books for both the trade and educational markets. She lives in New Fairfield, Connecticut.